AMERICA
The Beautiful Land

This book was devised and produced by
Multimedia Publications (UK) Ltd

Editor: Marilyn Inglis
Production: Arnon Orbach
Design: Terry Allen Associates
Picture Research: Virginia Landry

First published in the United States of America
1985 by Gallery Books, an imprint of W. H. Smith
Publishers Inc., 112 Madison Avenue, New York,
NY 10016.

ISBN 0 8317 0315 6

Typeset by Keene Graphics
Color origination by D. S. Colour International Ltd, London
Printed in Italy by New Interlitho, Milan

AMERICA
The Beautiful Land

Eric Inglefield

GALLERY BOOKS
An Imprint of W. H. Smith Publishers Inc.
112 Madison Avenue
New York City 10016

Contents

1

A Land of Contrasts

Left Sculpted in granite across the summit of 6000-ft Mount Rushmore, the portraits of four great American presidents — Washington, Jefferson, Theodore Roosevelt and Lincoln — rise above the forested landscapes of the Black Hills of South Dakota. This tremendous undertaking, the creation of Gutzon Borglum, was completed in 1941 after more than six years of work.

In 1927, at the age of 60, the sculptor Gutzon Borglum embarked upon the mammoth task of creating a huge monument to Presidents Washington, Jefferson, Theodore Roosevelt and Lincoln. Even more astonishingly, the monument was to consist of four 60 ft heads carved out of the granite summit of Mount Rushmore, in South Dakota's lovely pine-clad Black Hills. The product of Borglum's intensely-felt patriotism, the achievement — now known as the Shrine of Democracy — fulfilled his dream to shape "somewhere in America ... a few feet of stone that bears witness ... of the great things we accomplished as a nation, placed so high it won't pay to pull down for lesser purposes". Mount Rushmore is now one of America's most impressive and cherished national monuments.

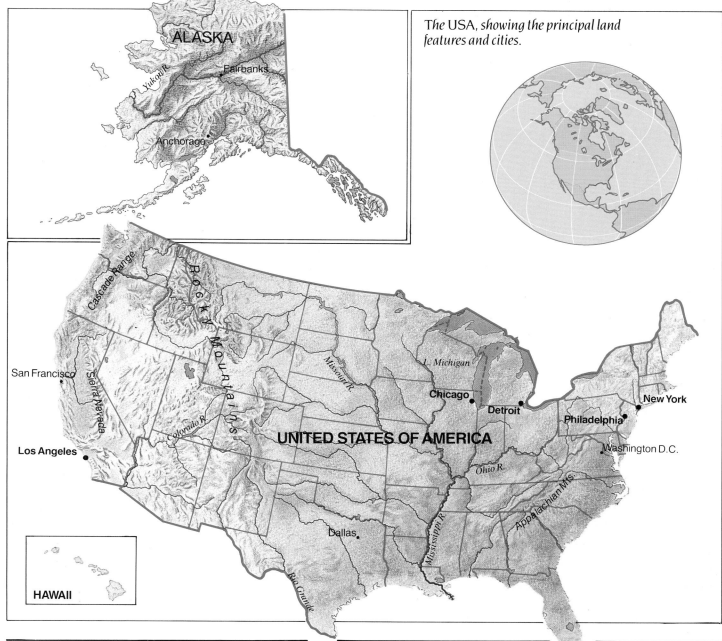

The USA, showing the principal land features and cities.

It is perhaps ironic that this magnificent tribute to American civilization, boldly gouged out of the beautiful landscape and visible for miles, stands in the heart of territory long held sacred by Sioux Indians. The Sioux were one of the indigenous Indian peoples dispossessed of their traditional homelands as white pioneer settlers spread relentlessly across the continent in the late eighteenth and nineteenth centuries.

The Indians did not regard themselves as owners of the land, which they could sell, buy, fence off and exploit for private gain, but as its temporary custodians, guarding a precious heritage for future generations. They saw their way of life as an integral part of the pattern of nature. As hunters and farmers they understood the behavior of wild animals and the properties of plants. They found explanations, interwoven with religion and legend, for distinctive features of the landscape and the various phenomena of the weather. Thus they handed down beautiful stories to account for the origin of the awesome 865 ft rock pillar called Devils Tower, which is a prominent landmark in the plains of Wyoming. Geologists now tell us, more prosaically, that it was formed by the cooling of molten rock in a vertical crack in the surrounding rocks, which were subsequently worn away by the elements to leave the harder pillar exposed.

Known to local Indians as Mateo Tepee, or Grizzly Bear Lodge, Devils Tower is one of countless sites in America endowed with lovely, often poetic, Indian names, many of them translated into English. Thus the map shows Sleeping Ute Mountain in Colorado, Lake Okeechobee (Big Water) in Florida, Kitch-Iti-Ki-Pi (Mirror of Heaven) Springs in Michigan, and the state of Minnesota (Sky-colored Waters), and many more. Early white settlers, too, invented tales to explain the breathtaking natural landmarks

Below Many Indian legends surround the mysterious Devils Tower, which rises abruptly from the Great Plains in Wyoming. According to one, seven young Indian girls, out one day in the pine woods, were attacked by a bear. Seeing their plight, the Great Spirit caused the land on which they were standing to rise like a tower. When the infuriated bear seemed about to claw its way to the top — hence the fluted ridges up the sides — the Great Spirit lifted the girls into the heavens and transformed them into the stars of the Pleiades.

Right The bald eagle, the official emblem of the United States, is a majestic white-headed bird of prey with a wing spread of 8ft. Most commonly seen in remote mountain areas and in Alaska, it nests high in trees or on rocky ledges near rivers or lakes, over which it often makes impressive swoops to catch large fish.

Above   The rich farmlands that cover around three-quarters of the state of Oklahoma mark the southernmost extent of the vast Central Plains region that stretches across the interior of the United States.

they encountered as they ventured into virgin territories, such as the legendary exploits of the giant Paul Bunyan and his blue ox, Babe, credited with the creation of many a landscape feature — even the Grand Canyon — as they stumbled across the country.

However, the advance of modern science has revealed the facts behind America's physical structure, yielding basic information and statistics, instead of poetic explanations. The United States covers an area of 3 615 122 square miles and is the world's fourth largest country after the Soviet Union, China and Canada; its entire coastline, including Alaska, stretches for 12 383 miles; its highest peak is 20 320-foot Mount McKinley in Alaska, and its lowest point is Badwater in California's Death Valley, 282 feet below sea level.

Modern geology has also revealed that, beneath the thick layers of rocks on the surface of continental America (excluding Alaska and Hawaii), lies a foundation of granite and other ancient rocks that breaks through to the surface near the Canadian border and in hilly areas such as the Black Hills of South Dakota and the Adirondacks of New York State. It also appears at the bottom of the mile-deep Grand Canyon cut by the Colorado River through the surface rocks of Arizona.

Below Vast herds of buffalo, or bison, once roamed the grasslands of the Great Plains and provided the Indians with hides and meat. In the nineteenth century, they were almost annihilated by white settlers during the bitter struggle with the Indians for control of the land, but are now recovering their numbers in protected areas such as Yellowstone National Park in Wyoming.

In the east and west of the continent, the surface rocks have been uplifted and folded into two great bands of mountains running roughly in a north-south direction; in the east are the Appalachians, with their ancient, deeply-eroded ridges and valleys, and in the west the much younger, higher, more rugged mountains and plateaux that include the lofty Rocky Mountains. The whole structure is like a giant hammock slung between two tree branches, the one to the east lower and thinner than the one to the west.

Over eons, great ice sheets have covered the extreme north and high mountains at various times, scraping and grinding their contours into rounded hills, deep hollows and broad, smooth valleys. As they retreated they left behind mounds of rock debris, vast areas of fertile soils, and thousands of cool, crystal lakes, including the Great Lakes.

The pervasive forces of erosion and weathering — mainly water (in the form of rain and rivers), ice, frost, wind and the sun's hot rays — have gradually shaped the surface features, while in Hawaii and the high plateaux of the West, volcanoes and lava flows have also contributed to the landscape, sometimes dramatically. Off the east coast and the Gulf of Mexico in the west, ocean currents have also created long low sandspits and shallow lagoons, while the mighty Mississippi River, with its many tributaries draining the interior plains region, has built a huge delta of silt far out into the sea at its mouth.

Nature has wrought a kaleidoscope of infinitely varied landscape, with a wide range of vegetation reflecting the spectrum of climate — from the cool, coniferous forests of the north to the hot cactus deserts of the southwest, from the grassy expanse of the Great Plains to the steaming cypress swamps of the southeast. In a land such as this, which provides a wide array of natural habitats, wild animals and plants abound in astonishing variety.

Over the last two hundred years the United States gained its independence from European domination, expanding across the North American continent from the Atlantic to the Pacific; farming, forestry, and

Right Fittingly named "The Last Frontier" of America, the bleak wilderness of Alaska is an awesome, yet beautiful, spectacle in the icy grip of winter. Mount Huntington is one of several towering peaks in the Alaska Range, which stretches across the southern part of the state and encloses the mountain wonderland of Denali National Park around Mount McKinley.

Below Zion National Park, a breathtaking scenic wonderland of massive rockfaces, canyons and buttes in southwestern Utah, has been shaped over millions of years by the relentless forces of erosion. Aided by the rain, wind and frost, the fast-flowing North Fork of the Virgin River has carved a spectacular canyon through the red and white sandstone rocks. Ebenezer Bryce, one of the first Mormon settlers in the area, drily commented that Zion was "a helluva place to lose a cow".

Festooned with the luxuriant tropical plants, the cool natural amphitheater known as the Fern Grotto is a well-known landmark on the Wailua River on the Hawaiian island of Kauai. At the center of this beautiful island, clothed in lush forest and exotic plants, is Mount Waialeale, the world's wettest place, which receives more than 500 inches of rain a year.

the construction of dams and vast cities have dramatically and irrevocably changed the landscape.

In the nineteenth century, however, many Americans came to realize there was a need to protect the nation's most spectacular natural wonders from commercial exploitation and possible destruction. With backing from such powerful national figures as President Theodore Roosevelt, the National Park system came into being, while many other areas were set aside as wildlife refuges. Today millions of people annually visit nearly 300 acres of scenic, geological, biological or historical interest in the National Park system scattered throughout the United States. It is perhaps fitting that a great monument to the Indian way of life, so perfectly in tune with nature itself, is now being carved from a mountainside in the Black Hills of South Dakota. It is a colossal mounted figure of the charismatic Sioux chief Crazy Horse, only a few miles from Gutzon Borglum's Shrine of Democracy.

So America remains a beautiful land with its splendid heritage of breathtaking natural scenery, rich profusion of wild plants and animals, and countless made-made wonders — beautiful buildings, bridges and monuments — enshrining its epic story.

Right The glittering mirror-glass towers of downtown Dallas rise abruptly from the Texas plains, their windows aflame in the red glow of sunset. Such bold modern skyscrapers are a feature of many American city centers as a result of the vast construction and revitalization programs in recent years.

Below The searing, inhospitable desert of Death Valley is a land of violent extremes. The land drops to America's lowest point — 282 ft below sea level — and summer temperatures soar well above 100F, once reaching a record 134F.

2

Landscapes

Left *Described by Herman Melville in Moby Dick as "a mere hillock and elbow of sand", the old whaling-port island of Martha's Vineyard is part of the Northeast's submerged coastal plain, which also includes Nantucket, Long Island and Cape Cod. Gay Head, at the southwest tip of the island, is a well-known landmark.*

Below *Normally lashed by the thundering surf of the Atlantic Ocean, the windswept Schoodic Peninsula, on Maine's wild rugged coast, is sometimes a scene of quiet beauty. The peninsula is the only mainland section of Acadia National Park, which offers magnificent vistas.*

Around the middle of the nineteenth century, thousands of Americans and newly-arrived immigrants living in the cities and on the farms of the Eastern States set off for unknown territories beyond the Mississippi River in response to the persuasive call "Go West, young man!" The breathtaking landscapes they found in the West have long impressed travelers, among them no less a figure than President Theodore Roosevelt himself, who, on a visit to Colorado in 1901, exclaimed in admiration, "The scenery bankrupts the English language."

Few countries can boast such an astonishing variety of beautiful natural scenery, much of it still unspoiled by the advance of modern civilization. There are towering mountain ranges and snow-clad volcanoes, remote wildernesses and glaciers, dense evergreen forests and subtropical jungles, sagebrush plateaux and baking deserts, rolling grasslands and multicolored checkerboards of fields.

In the early seventeenth century, the first English, Dutch and Swedish settlers established colonies on the deeply-indented east coast, with its tidal river estuaries and offshore islands which afforded suitable harbors for the pioneer communities. In the north, in present-day New England,

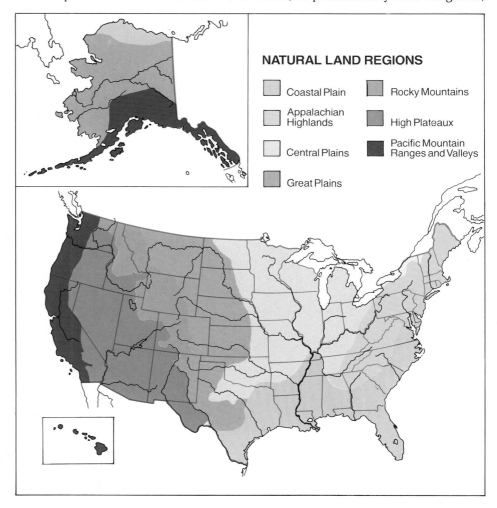

NATURAL LAND REGIONS

- Coastal Plain
- Appalachian Highlands
- Central Plains
- Great Plains
- Rocky Mountains
- High Plateaux
- Pacific Mountain Ranges and Valleys

the ice-worn granite hilltops, glacial lakes and rocky promontories of Acadia National Park and the windswept sand dunes of hook-like Cape Cod represent the timeless wild beauty of this magnificent shoreline.

Farther south, beyond the Hudson River valley and New York City, the coastal plain begins to broaden and the long tidal inlets of Delaware and Chesapeake Bays slice across its green farmland. Offshore, ocean currents have thrown up long, thread-like sandspits far out to sea, among them the remote world of mountainous sand dunes, mud flats and marshes in North Carolina's Outer Banks.

The coastal plain extends southward into the flat Florida peninsula and then turns west along the great curve of the Gulf of Mexico. Behind the shoreline, with its lagoons and sand bars, are immense reed marshes and cypress swamps teeming with wild animals. The best known include Georgia's wild Marshes of Glynn and nearby Okefenokee Swamp, the famous Everglades, south Florida's subtropical wildlife paradise, and the steamy bayou country around the mouth of the Mississippi River in Louisiana.

Previous Page The beautiful countryside of Vermont, in the northern reaches of the Appalachian Mountains, is a scenic tapestry of soft green meadows with varying textures and hues of maples, birch and many other kinds of trees. Here and there, colorful clapboard buildings and gleaming white steeples attract the eye.

Above Right Once a saltwater inlet of the Atlantic Ocean, the mysterious and fascinating Okefenokee Swamp now covers 681 square miles of southern Georgia. Over much of its area bald cypress trees festooned with Spanish moss rise eerily from the water, while in the eastern parts there are great open "prairies" of water lilies cut by "runs" used by swamp boats.

Right From here at Newfound Gap, it is easy to see how this magnificent Appalachian wilderness, enclosed in the Great Smoky Mountains National Park, got its colorful name.

Down the eastern side of the United States, the forested ridges and cultivated valleys of the Appalachians form a broad band of spectacular mountain scenery from Maine in the north to Alabama in the south. In New England the mountains are broken up by river valleys into distinct sections that include the Green Mountains, the Berkshires and the White Mountains, where the bleak summit of Mount Washington, the highest point in the region, rises to 6288 feet. Long ago, immense glaciers covered this land and shaped a landscape of bare, rounded mountain tops, steep-sided valleys, clear, sparkling lakes and scattered mounds of rock debris, a scenic wonderland now covered with forests and meadows and drained by fast-flowing streams.

The southern part of the Appalachians also embraces the Blue Ridge Mountains of Virginia in Shenandoah National Park, where the spectacular Skyline Drive overlooks the farming country of the Shenandoah Valley. Farther south, the summits of the Great Smoky Mountains rise above their green mantle of forest, permanently wrapped in a delicate blue haze. Here Mount Mitchell reaches 6684 feet, the highest point east of the Mississippi River. Along the eastern side of the Appalachians the land slopes down to the Atlantic coastal plain across the ancient rocks of the Piedmont Plateau, at the edge of which the rivers plunge over the fall line in boulder-strewn, whitewater rapids. Many of the east coast's major cities are located along this line, including Philadelphia, Baltimore, Washington D.C. and Richmond.

Right Rocky bluffs hundreds of feet high, thick forests and thundering cascades line the north shore of Lake Superior in northeastern Minnesota. The magnificent scenic highway that runs along the remote shoreline from the port of Duluth passes many impressive sights.

Below Despite the tawdry commercialism that now surrounds them Niagara Falls remain one of the most impressive natural wonders in the world. Created by the Niagara River as it flows from Lake Erie into Lake Ontario, the falls are particularly exciting when viewed from one of the daring little tourist boats which ply at their base.

West of the Appalachians the land slopes down the Allegheny and Cumberland plateaux into the vast interior plains that stretch for 1000 miles as far as the Rocky Mountains. From the woodlands of Ohio, Kentucky and Tennessee, a brown, green and gold checkerboard of plains sweeps westward across the country as far as Nebraska and Kansas. This section, known as the Central Plains, is America's agricultural heartland and extends from the Great Lakes in the north to the plains bordering the Gulf of Mexico in the south. The monotony of this generally flat or gently rolling landscape is, however, broken by several hilly areas of outstanding scenic interest. Chief among these is the beautiful limestone country of the Ozark Plateau in Missouri and Arkansas, with its rushing rivers, deep gorges, springs and underground caverns. In the far north, in Minnesota, Wisconsin and Michigan, the farm belt gives way to a landscape of thick forests, glacial lakes and low mountain ranges. The untamed beauty of this remote wilderness area, with its abundant wildlife, is now preserved in Voyageurs National Park, Boundary Waters Canoe Area and Isle Royale National Park, on a lovely island in Lake Superior.

Previous Page The Badlands of South Dakota emerge from the open prairies like a moonscape of rugged beauty. Here the elements have molded weird pinnacles, sharp ridges and deep ravines in the soft layers of multicolored rock.

Below One of the most photographed groups of mountains in America, the magnificent Grand Tetons, in northwestern Wyoming, are endowed with additional beauty when snow blankets the 13 000 ft peaks and the flat valley of Jackson Hole in a glistening white mantle. This outstanding wildlife wonderland, crossed by the winding Snake River, is enclosed in Grand Teton National Park.

Right At Mammoth Hot Springs, in the northern part of Yellowstone National Park, white travertine terraces have been built up where hot water laden with minerals wells up from deep below ground. Like a giant staircase designed for the gods, the Minerva Terrace is a particularly impressive feature of this thermal area.

Below The slopes of Colorado's Rocky Mountains are a major attraction for skiing enthusiasts. The pleasant old silver-mining town of Aspen is one of many resorts in the state offering excellent facilities, crisp, dry, powder snow and clear blue skies.

Starting as a trickle from tiny Lake Itasca in Minnesota's forests, the mighty Mississippi, principal river of the whole interior plains region, flows for 2552 miles on its journey to the Gulf of Mexico, its course joined by many other great rivers. From the west comes the Missouri, affectionately nicknamed "Big Muddy", the Arkansas, Red and other rivers; from the Appalachians to the east flow the Ohio and Tennessee rivers, the latter tamed by several dams to create lovely lake scenery amid Tennessee's mountains. Each river passes through scenery of incomparable beauty, while the Mississippi itself, in its upper reaches, boasts a particularly magnificent stretch of rugged, tree-covered bluffs known as the Palisades. After meandering through the fertile farmlands of the South, the "Father of Waters" finally enters the sea through its immense delta, the flat bayou country, site of the colorful old city port of New Orleans.

31

Left The rock feature known as Delicate Arch rises as high as a seven-story building above the surrounding red sandstone cliffs in southern Utah's Arches National Park. Smoothed into this extraordinary shape over time by rain, wind and frost, the arch is the most famous landmark in the park and one of over 90 such arches so far discovered.

Left Aptly described in the local Indian name as "red rocks standing like men in a bowl," Bryce Canyon, in southern Utah, is a remarkable spectacle of massed red and white pinnacles sculpted in soft rock by the forces of erosion. The easy walk along the canyon rim between Sunrise and Sunset Points provides marvelous views of the formations down below.

Right The best-known and most visited geyser in Yellowstone National Park is Old Faithful, which regularly shoots a spectacular plume of hot water 130 ft into the air at intervals of around 70 minutes. In the same area are several other geysers, each different from the others in the height, duration and frequency of their eruptions.

West of the Central Plains the land rises across the drier open grasslands region of the Great Plains, a band of territory some 300-500 miles wide which rises to about 5000 feet on the edge of the Rocky Mountains. Here Denver has gradually become the major city of the region. Once misleadingly dubbed the "Great American Desert" by early explorers, the Great Plains are now covered by vast wheatlands and cattle ranches, wide-open expanses in which the trees generally cluster along the rivers. There are also many areas and sites of scenic appeal, including the lovely forested Black Hills and weird Badlands of the Dakotas, the awesome Devils Tower in Wyoming, and many fascinating rock outcrops and formations in Nebraska and Kansas.

Below Perhaps the most awesome spectacle in the world, the Grand Canyon, in northern Arizona, is an indescribable landscape of chasms, rock buttes and flat plateaux. The canyon, 277 miles long and up to 18 miles wide, has been gouged through the multicolored rock layers by the Colorado River which is now carving through some of the oldest rocks on earth.

Above *Against the glow of sunset, armies of giant saguaro cacti march across the Sonoran desert in southern Arizona. These remarkable plants are protected in Saguaro National Monument near the city of Tucson.*

The Great Plains come to a sudden halt where the towering wall of the Rocky Mountains looms up on the western horizon. Throughout the Rockies, the mountain scenery is spectacular, particularly in those areas designated as National Parks. Astride Montana's border with Canada is Glacier National Park, a rugged wilderness of towering ridges and precipitous rockfaces, glaciers and crystal-clear lakes; Wyoming offers Yellowstone National Park, with its hot springs, mud pools and geysers, and Grand Teton National Park, with its spectacular uplifted block of soaring craggy peaks; Colorado's Rocky Mountain National Park has breathtaking panoramas and majestic peaks rising to 14 000 ft.

In Wyoming, a break in the Rocky Mountains barrier permits the Great Plains to extend westward through a series of dry, scrubby basins into the high plateau region beyond. Stretching from Washington State in the north right down to the Mexican border, this band contains some of America's most outstanding scenic wonders. Its northern section, the Columbia Plateau, extends across parts of Washington, Oregon and Idaho, a land of volcanic lava flows and cinder cones, rich wheatlands, and deep gorges carved by the Columbia and Snake rivers. Farther south, the arid Great Basin, or Basin and Range Region, covers most of Nevada and parts of adjoining states. Here the landscape is dominated by parallel ridges of mountains, flat burning deserts, shimmering salt flats, and small rivers that peter out in desert "sinks". Here too is the Great Salt Lake of Utah, the reduced salty remnant of a much larger ancient lake.

Far Left More than 800 ft beneath the dry foothills of the Guadalupe Mountains in southern New Mexico, a succession of breathtaking sights awaits the visitor to Carlsbad Caverns. A series of huge underground chambers, the largest 255 ft high and covering 14 acres, contains an illuminated display of rock formations created by dripping water over millions of years. The caverns are also the home of millions of bats, which emerge on summer evenings to hunt for food.

Below Only the toughest of drought-resistant plants can survive in the hot, arid terrain of White Sands National Monument in southern New Mexico. This area of white gypsum dunes is some 30 miles long and 10 miles wide, a beautiful sight against the backdrop of distant mountains and clear blue sky.

Below Mount Rainier looms on the horizon amid the forest scenery of the Cascade Range in Washington State. With its dazzling glaciers, abundant wild animals and varied plant life, the 14 410 ft long-dormant volcano, has been fittingly designated a national park.

Right In the mountain and desert country of western Texas, the Rio Grande has cut a series of dramatic canyons with sheer-sided walls up to 1500 feet high through the pink and white rocks of Big Bend National Park. Despite the harshness of the terrain and the extremes of hot and cold, the park is a wonderland of desert wildlife.

Below *Before its eruption in May 1980, Mount St Helens, in the Cascade Range of Washington state, was a classic cone-shaped volcano. Today, with 1400 feet blasted off its summit the 8300 ft mountain stands with its crater gaping at the sky, a reminder of the earth's immense pent-up energy.*

To the south and east, in Colorado and Utah, the Colorado Plateau descends into the Great Basin from the edge of the Rockies, drained by the Colorado and other rivers. In places its stark, rugged surface is gashed by steep-sided canyons carved by these rivers, none more dramatic than the awesome Black Canyon of the Gunnison River. With its immense flat-topped *mesas*, towering buttes and multicolored rock formations, this geological wonderland boasts some of the most stunning sights in all America. Much of its staggering beauty is enclosed in a galaxy of National Parks: Arches, Bryce Canyon, Canyonlands, Capitol Reef, Zion and, most spectacular of all, the mile-deep Grand Canyon. In this region too is Monument Valley, whose towering chimneys of volcanic rock have provided a familiar backdrop for many a Western movie.

The Great Basin and Colorado Plateau extend into the southwestern states bordering Mexico — Arizona, New Mexico, and parts of California and Texas, where the visitor can marvel at yet more scenic splendors. Arizona's highlights include the strange Petrified Forest, the badlands of the Painted Desert, the spectacular Canyon de Chelly, Sunset Crater, and

At sunset, the granite rockface of Half Dome, in California's Yosemite National Park, is softened with pink tints. This majestic 8852 ft summit overlooks the Yosemite Valley, a mile-wide natural garden lined with impressive rock peaks and waterfalls.

the tracts of cacti protected in two National Monument areas: Saguaro and Organ Pipe Cactus. New Mexico has the remarkable Carlsbad Caverns and the White Sands National Monument, while western Texas boasts the rugged grandeur of the Guadalupe Mountains and Big Bend National Parks. To the west, in the lonely, bare desert of aptly named Death Valley are to be found the hottest, driest and lowest places in America, set amid vistas of unparalleled beauty just north of the immense expanse of the Mojave Desert.

West of the high plateau region, the Pacific coast states of Washington, Oregon and California are linked by the north-south mountain barrier formed by the Cascade Range and Sierra Nevada. In the north, snow-capped volcanic peaks, among them Rainier, Adams, Baker and now-devastated St Helens, soar above the landscape of the Cascades. Farther south, the magnificent Sierra Nevada embraces the glistening blue jewel of Lake Tahoe, the 14 495 ft peak of Mount Whitney, and the grandeur of Yosemite National Park, a stunningly beautiful landscape of colossal granite rockfaces, domes and tumbling high waterfalls.

Still relatively unspoiled by modern civilization, the magnificent Big Sur coast of southern California is a kaleidoscope of headlands, cliffs, islands, bays and meadows speckled with wild flowers. Along the shoreline live many sea birds, seals, sea lions and sea otters.

Between these mountains and the Coast Ranges flanking the Pacific shoreline is a series of broad, flat cultivated valleys — the Puget Sound lowland in Washington, Willamette Valley in Oregon and the immense Valley of California, where much of America's fruit and vegetable produce is grown. On the seaward side, the Coast Ranges run from the rain-soaked Olympic Mountains in the north to the drier ridges that form a backdrop to the great cities of Los Angeles and San Diego. Along this southern section runs the dreaded San Andreas Fault, with its constant threat of earthquakes. The shoreline itself, with its sandy beaches, rocky headlands and steep cliffs, has a special scenic magnificence, particularly in Oregon and along the Big Sur coast of southern California.

Far to the north, the immense state of Alaska encompasses a lonely wilderness of frozen tundra, magnificent ice-capped mountain ranges, impressive glaciers and dense forests. In the midst of its unforgettable landscapes rises the majestic peak of 20320 ft Mount McKinley, America's highest mountain, which soars above the wild surroundings of Denali National Park. Alaska provides a stark contrast with the subtropical islands of Hawaii, a paradise of golden beaches and lush vegetation halfway across the Pacific Ocean. Exceptional mountain scenery, still-active volcanoes and rugged coastlines give these islands their special enchantment, a legacy of beauty now preserved in two outstanding National Parks: Haleakala, on the island of Maui, and Hawaii Volcanoes, on Hawaii itself.

Right A flow of white-hot lava snaking down the slopes of the Mauna Loa volcano is a reminder that the lush-forested islands of Hawaii sit on top of awesome subterranean forces. During its periodic eruptions, 13 680 ft Mauna Loa can spew out great volumes of lava, which sometimes reach the sea in great clouds of steam.

Below From the comfort and safety of a cruise boat or sightseeing airplane, travelers to Alaska's Glacier Bay can watch as huge chunks of ice plunge into the sea from the towering face of glaciers.

3

Seasons

One of the fascinating things about the climate of the United States is that in the depth of winter, when northern cities may be freezing under a blanket of snow, Miami and Florida's vacation resorts may be basking in temperatures in the 70s. Similarly, Las Vegas may be baking in summer temperatures topping 100°F, while San Francisco, on almost the same latitude, remains cool in the comfortable 70s. America may be hot, cold, dry and wet all at the same time.

Because the United States is such a vast country, the usual moderating effects of the oceans cannot penetrate as far as the interior. This is emphasized further by the presence of the north-south mountain ranges in the West, which act as a barrier to movements of air across them. As a result, the high plateaux between the mountains and the Great Plains on the eastern side are deprived of rain. In addition, the central part of the country has to endure great extremes of temperature as bitterly cold air sweeps down from the Arctic in winter and hot, humid air moves up from the Caribbean in summer. At this time of year, also, violent thunderstorms, "twisters" (tornadoes) and even devastating hurricanes occur.

With such great variations in climatic conditions across the United States at any one time of the year, the seasons mean different things in

Annual rainfall in the United States. In general, the rainfall increases from the Rocky Mountains towards the southeast and northwest: the driest areas are the desert regions of the southwest. In winter, much of the precipitation falls in the form of snow in the north and in the mountainous areas.

Left *In spring and early summer a bright green carpet of trilliums, wood sorrel and other plants covers the forest floor in the northern Appalachians.*

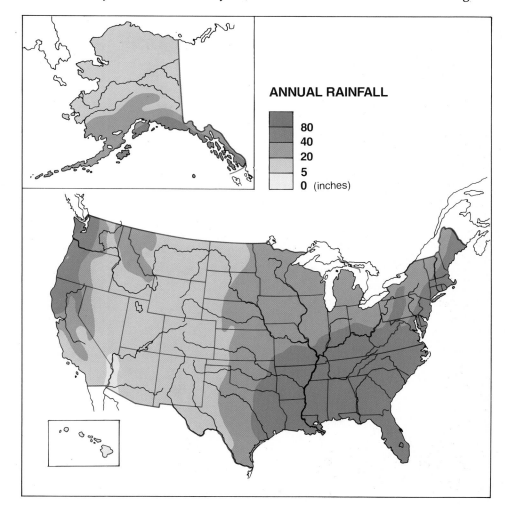

ANNUAL RAINFALL

80
40
20
5
0 (inches)

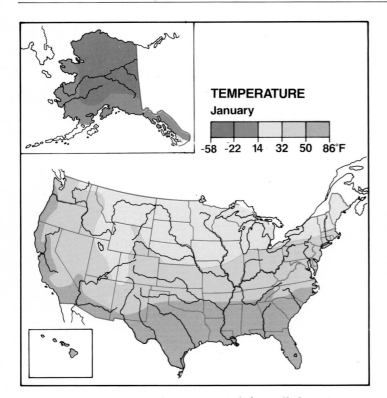

TEMPERATURE
January

-58 -22 14 32 50 86°F

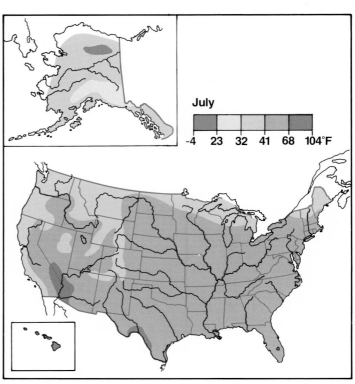

July

-4 23 32 41 68 104°F

Temperatures in January decrease toward the Gulf of Mexico as cold air masses move down from the Arctic. The Pacific Coast, however, is sheltered by the high mountain ranges inland.

Temperatures in July reach their peak in the deserts of the southwest, with the high mountains and the Pacific Coast remaining comparatively cooler.

Left A heartening springtime sight in the mountains and woodlands of the eastern states is the lovely dogwood. According to legend, the dogwood was used to make the cross for the Crucifixion, and its white flower bracts now bear torn, brown-stained tips caused by the rusty nails.

Right When warm days arrive to banish the rains of winter, the Sonoran Desert of Arizona explodes into a riot of color as brilliant yellow poppies carpet the land beneath the taller desert plants. Among these is the distinctive saguaro cactus which, after dusk, opens beautiful white blooms that last only a few hours.

different places. Frost-free southern Florida and Hawaii have no winter in the sense that other states do, and Alaska's cool summer, with its long hours of daylight, would be regarded as the equivalent of spring elsewhere in America. In some areas, winter bursts suddenly into summer, and vice versa, while in others there are four distinct seasons, each with its own special beauty.

In the more northerly parts of the United States and on the mountain slopes, the warm breath of spring loosens winter's icy grip as it banishes the last patches of snow and entices buds to unfurl into life. Forests of sombre, bare trees dress their twiggy branches in a flimsy gauze of cheerful green, and the first spring flowers brighten the landscape with gaudy splashes of color. In the Appalachians, redbuds and dogwoods, followed by flame azaleas, mountain laurels and rhododendrons respond to the lengthening days with exuberant showers of blossom, while lovely painted trilliums, lady's slippers and countless other wild flowers stud the forested hillsides and meadows in colorful profusion.

Across the vast plains, shoots of new prairie grass emerge from last year's dry tinder as male sharptail grouse and prairie chickens begin their age-old ritual dance for the favor of watching hens. Up on the desert plateaux of the West a similar courtship routine is performed by the remarkable sage grouse, and across the entire country birds begin the frantic business of finding a mate, building a nest and raising their young. For this purpose many birds fly in from warmer regions along the well-established migration routes, or "flyways", that criss-cross the country from north to south. At the same time, others, such as Nebraska's sandhill cranes, fly off to breeding grounds in the far northern wildernesses of Canada. Hibernating animals, among them squirrels, muskrats and other small rodents, stir from their winter slumber to restart the annual cycle of life.

Far Left Long-legged wading birds, such as herons and egrets, can often be seen outlined against the afterglow on summer evenings as they fly back to their roosting sites in the marshes and lagoons of Florida and the Gulf of Mexico.

Left Florida is better known for its Left America is a bounteous country and here in the Midwest fertile soil provides a generous crop to add to the nation's grain stores during the long hot summer months.

As spring turns into summer, the green of the forests and meadows is at its most luxuriant, and wild creatures everywhere feed on the available bounty while the season lasts. As the weeks pass, and the days become hot and sultry, the grasslands and wheatfields of the heartland slowly turn to endless oceans of gold. In the deserts and mountain plateaux of the West, the shimmering heat creates a mirage effect of water across the parched flat expanses, and temperatures in Death Valley soar into the 100s. At this time of year, cool morning mists roll in from the Pacific over northern California's shoreline, creating an eerie atmosphere among the redwoods and in the streets of San Francisco. On the plains and high plateaux to the east, relief from the heat comes in late summer with tremendous thunderstorms that turn the dry creeks into raging torrents, the dark skies creating a dramatic backdrop to the red and gold landscapes.

Summer declines into the cooler days of fall, and spiders' webs greet the morning sun with their pearly dewdrops. The forests and woodlands across the country now take on mellower tints of brown, gold and red. Few autumn spectacles surpass the beauty of New England as the maples and other forest trees turn the hillsides into flame. Vying with them, however, are the aspens and riverside cottonwoods that glow with gold beneath the clear blue skies of the mountains in the West.

The first snows of winter begin to drive elk and other mountain animals from the lush high meadows into lower valleys, such as Jackson Hole, in Wyoming. On the plains, as the grain elevators fill up with the golden harvest, storms sweep across Montana and the Dakotas from the north, bringing a foretaste of the coming winter with their flurries of snow. Now the majestic greater snow geese pass in massed squadrons over New York to winter along the salt marshes of the eastern seaboard, just one of the many species of birds to fly down from the north at this time.

Right and Below B*asking in the warmth of the summer sun, the Californian poppy creates a swaying carpet on grassy hillsides. Now the state flower, it once grew so abundantly that early Spanish colonists called this part of America the "Golden West."*

Left The brilliant fall colors of trees are the result of chemical changes inside the leaves. With the approach of cooler days, the production of green chlorophyll gradually stops and yellow and red pigments begin to appear in its place. Waste products called tannins also tint some leaves brown.

Above With the arrival of the cooler, shorter days of autumn, the forests of Wisconsin and other northern states are transformed into a patchwork of red, orange, yellow and brown foliage, a sight equalled only by the magnificent display of fall colors in New England.

Many wild animals, fattened in preparation for their long winter sleep, curl up in burrows to outlive the frost. Others have different methods of survival, such as the amazing monarch butterflies that fly off to Mexico. There are also the buffalo and other animals that gather to graze in the comparative warmth created by the hot springs and geysers in Wyoming's Yellowstone National Park. As winter tightens its grip, Alaska retreats into its bleak, long winter nights. In the mountains and northern parts of the rest of the country, snow casts a shroud of pure white over the landscape, and ponds freeze over to the delight of adventurous youngsters. During these months, gray whales can be seen off the Californian coast as they migrate to warm breeding grounds farther south in Mexican waters.

Oblivious to these dramatic seasonal changes elsewhere, vacationers and residents in southern Florida and Hawaii bask in the warm winter sunshine on palm-fringed sandy beaches.

Right Although snow may be beautiful when seen from the comfort of a warm fireside, it is no fun for man or beast to be caught in a blizzard when far from home.

Far Right A pattern of ice blocks in Rockport Harbor, Massachusetts, is the handiwork of the New England winter, which not only covers the land with snow but also freezes the water of the sea in coastal harbors.

Below Under snow, the scenery of Yosemite National Park in California takes on a different beauty. Then the park's massive rock fortresses have an ethereal quality as they alternately emerge and vanish amid the low, swirling clouds.

4

Plants and Animals

The wild plants and animals of the United States are just as varied and fascinating as its scenic wonders. The diversity of land and climatic regions offers a wide range of suitable habitats for all kinds of living things.

Over the years, human beings have had an influence on the pattern of wildlife throughout the United States, sometimes with devastating results. In the nineteenth century vast herds of buffalo were slaughtered by white settlers and hunters, and the lovely passenger pigeon shot to extinction. The development of land for farming and other uses also changed natural habitats, notably in the Midwest corn belt.

Yet there have also been beneficial aspects to this development. Reservoirs built in arid parts of the United States, for example, have created new natural environments in which groups of interdependent animals and plants can thrive. The reservoirs support not only fish and other freshwater life but also fish-eating birds and water-loving animals.

As people have become more conscious of the need to conserve America's great natural heritage, many areas of the United States with particularly interesting animal and plant life have been set aside as wildlife refuges or placed under the protection of the National Parks Service, providing fascinating opportunities for nature lovers to marvel at America's rich collection of living things.

One of the most curious and primitive of America's wild creatures is the strange horseshoe crab, which appears in great numbers along New England's beaches during the spring breeding season. Its eggs are a welcome delicacy for the many gulls and other sea birds that inhabit this rugged coast. The whole Atlantic shoreline, with its cliffs, sand dunes, salt marshes, tidal inlets and lagoons, offers a choice of natural habitats for a wide assortment of birds. Among them are fish crows, egrets, herons, noisy clapper rails, redwings, bitterns, numerous ducks and snow geese. Of particular interest along this coast are the wild Chincoteague ponies that roam over Assateague Island.

In North Carolina is the Dismal Swamp, a place rich in wildlife described by the poet Longfellow:

> Where will-o-the-wisps and glow worms shine,
> In bulrush and in brake;
> Where waning masses shroud the pine
> And the cedar grows, and the poisonous vine
> Is spotted like the snake.

Another of the South's famous wetlands is the Okefenokee Swamp, in Georgia, where cypress trees draped in Spanish moss rise from waters teeming with fish, frogs, snapping turtles and various water snakes, none more deadly than the fearsome cottonmouth. Everywhere there are birds, especially herons and elegant whooping cranes.

Farther south, the Everglades of Florida are another wildlife paradise, with expanses of saw grass dotted with mangroves and islands of hardwood trees, palms and exotic plants. Apart from its famous alligators, this natural garden has many other kinds of reptiles, amphibians, butterflies and lovely birds, such as the snowy egret, wood ibis, anhinga (or snake bird), various herons and the iridescent purple gallinule.

The great egret is a graceful, long-legged wading bird seen in all parts of the world in both fresh and saltwater marshes and lakes, where it feeds on fish, frogs and other water creatures. In the breeding season it courts its mate by displaying decorative plumes, or "aigrettes," along its back. These need careful and regular preening.

Many of the same species of birds frequent the coastal islands, lagoons and bayous of the Gulf of Mexico, where Padre Island, in Texas, is a special attraction for bird-watchers. This coast is also the home of the whooping crane, brown pelican, avocet, roseate spoonbill and other exotic birds, as well as the large rat-like coypu and a strange amphibian known as the siren.

North of the pine woods that extend across the lowlands of the southern states, the Appalachian Mountains are clothed in a green mantle of forest of mostly deciduous trees in the south and of conifers on the higher slopes in New England. The deciduous trees are mainly oak, hickory, maple, walnut and dogwood, while in the undergrowth wild flowers and smaller shrubs, such as rhododendrons and mountain laurel, splash the scenery with seasonal color. Among these forests live many wild creatures, including the raccoon, opossum, skunk and the solitary porcupine. Other favorites with nature lovers are the hard-working beaver, the fisher marten, the chipmunk and, often to be seen rummaging in trash cans by the wayside, the black bear. Flitting among the trees are such colorful birds as the kingfisher, scarlet tanager, blue jay and cardinal, while in the streams lurk the ugly hellbender salamander.

Right *Bald cypress trees growing from a tangle of exposed sturdy roots are a common sight along creeks and in swamps in the South and Southeast. They are not true cypresses, which are evergreen, but lose their leaves every fall, hence their name.*

Below *The beautiful monarch butterfly, with its unmistakable reddish-brown, black and white wings, is widespread throughout the United States. Unlike most other butterflies, monarchs migrate south in the fall to the California coast or to Mexico, where they gather in large masses to breed. In spring, the young butterflies replace their parents by flying north.*

Deciduous woodlands cover the western side of the Appalachians. Farther west, the rich farmlands of the Central Plains, once rolling grasslands, are the home of beavers, long-tailed weasels, mink and many other animals. Kestrels, ducks and gamebirds, such as the wild turkey, grouse and pheasant, are also common. In the rivers and ponds live all kinds of freshwater fish, among them the strange paddlefish (or spoonbill) and mud puppy.

A much wider range of animals inhabits the wilder, forested hilly parts of the Central Plains. In the Ozarks live large numbers of deer, rabbits and squirrels. At night, when raccoons and opossums are out wandering, the silence of the darkness is sometimes pierced by the scream of a bobcat or the eerie hooting of an owl. Yet the most spine-chilling night sounds of all are those heard in the remote forest wildernesses of northern Minnesota, where the howl of the timber wolf and the insane cackle of the loon echo to the accompanying soft whistle of the wind.

The open plain of southwestern Minnesota is home to the little burrowing rodent that earned the state its nickname 'The Gopher State'. It is one of many fascinating animals that also inhabit the Great Plains to the west. Once roamed by immense herds of buffalo, this vast grassland region, crossed by rivers and creeks lined with cottonwoods, is the habitat of the prairie chicken, pronghorn, coyote and badger. Here, too, live the black-footed ferret and its prey, the delightful prairie dog, which sits on its haunches by its burrow and barks like a dog when danger threatens. Among the many kinds of grasses that grow on the plains are hosts of beautiful wild flowers, especially the sunflower, state flower of Kansas.

Previous Page *The tree frog is well adapted to climbing trees by having adhesive pads on its toes. Because its color is an effective camouflage, it has little fear when handled. There are several species in the eastern and southern parts of the country.*

Left *The grasslands of Oklahoma and other southwestern states are covered in spring and summer with wildflowers. One of the brightest is the Indian Blanket, an annual species of gaillardia with attractive yellow and red daisy-like flowers that grow up to 2 ft high.*

Right *The clouded sulfur butterfly is found all over the United States, its yellow-green wings adding a splash of color to the countryside. Like all butterflies, it feeds on the nectar produced by flowers, which it sucks up through its unfurled proboscis.*

62

Left Because of its ability to regulate its body temperature, the gopher tortoise can survive in the hot desert regions of the West and Southwest. After a period of time basking in the sun, it then hides in long burrows up to 10 ft below ground in order to cool off and reduce the loss of water from its body.

Right The giant saguaro is a remarkable plant of the Arizona desert that grows up to 50 ft high and lives for up to 200 years. The waxy, orange-centered white flowers appear in clusters at the ends of branches in May and June every year, but each one lasts for less than a day.

Below Like other species of rattlesnake in the United States, the prairie, or western, rattlesnake has a horny set of rings at the end of its tail which it rattles as a warning to an intruder. Small depressions beneath its eyes enable it to detect heat radiated by other animals.

Right Named for the spiny scales on its cones, the bristlecone pine grows among the arid mountain regions of the West. Some gnarled specimens, although only around 30 ft tall, are thought to be about 4000 years old. Ghostly white branches seen on many bristlecones are the somber evidence of their struggle to survive in the harsh conditions.

Below The delightful little chipmunk can be seen in daylight hours running about in short, nervous bursts as it forages for food. Several kinds of chipmunk, including the lodgepole chipmunk, inhabit the West, while a larger species is found in the eastern states.

On the western edge of the Great Plains, stands of ponderosa pine, Douglas fir and spruce climb the slopes of the Rocky Mountains, supplanted higher up by clumps of lodgepole pine and aspen, while above the tree line, spring flowers brighten the alpine meadows. In this rugged landscape stalk the puma, or mountain lion, the bobcat, and grizzly and black bears. Underground, in its burrow, hides the yellow-bellied marmot, while bighorn sheep, moose and wapiti graze peacefully overhead. Various species of eagle and hawk hover in the clear mountain skies, scanning for an unwary pika or other tasty small prey.

In the parched plateaux west of the Rockies, forests of ponderosa pine and other conifers clothe many of the mountain ridges, where occasional bristlecone pines, piñons and junipers cling to bare rockfaces. Flat scrubby valleys of sagebrush, mesquite and creosote gradually merge into the desert country of the Southwest, where the stately saguaro cactus, prickly pear, cholla cactus and other drought-resistant plants, such as the

Left The puma, also known as the mountain lion or cougar, is an excellent hunter. Although frequently hunted by ranchers, the puma rarely takes domestic animals and is really quite timid.

Right Groves of giant sequoia trees, now protected in Sequoia and Kings Canyon National Parks, clothe the western slopes of the Sierra Nevada in California. Some of these magnificent trees are thousands of years old and have been given the names of famous people in American history. The General Sherman tree, for example, is 275 ft tall and measures 103 ft round the trunk.

Joshua tree, dot the parched landscape. In this inhospitable territory an astonishing assortment of wild creatures manage to survive, among them many lizards, including huge gila monsters, deadly rattlesnakes, scorpions and desert tortoises. Small mammals also abound, including skunks, comic jack rabbits with their huge ears, agile cacomistles, or ring-tailed cats, cotton-tails, pack rats and pocket mice. Some birds in these desert regions, such as cactus wrens, elf owls and gila woodpeckers, even nest among the spiny branches of tall cacti.

Succulent desert plants also thrive in sunny southern California, where native Washingtonia palms and eucalyptus trees introduced from Australia are also widespread. Among the exotic wild creatures of this part of America are majestic California condors, white-winged doves and tiny, exquisite, iridescent hummingbirds, and such mammals as spotty-coated ocelots, a type of raccoon called coatimundi, and the rare jaguar.

To the north, on the western slopes of the Sierra Nevada, grow the magnificent giant sequoias that attract large numbers of visitors to Sequoia and Kings Canyon National Parks. Farther north still, coniferous trees — spruce, fir, hemlock and pine — mantle the slopes of the volcano-studded Cascade Range. To the northwest, on Washington State's mountainous Olympic Peninsula, is an eerie world of moss-draped rain forest, luxuriant ferns and fungi, where elk and deer wander silently through the gloom.

Right *Lush green ferns and other plants thrive in the moist environment along the coast of northern California.*

Below *Dressed in its iridescent colors, Rivoli's hummingbird is one of several kinds of small hummingbirds that live in the warm regions of the West.*

5

Man-Made Creations

When discussing American history, most people begin with the founding of the 13 original English colonies in the early seventeenth century. Yet the story goes back long before that — more than 25 000 years, in fact. It was in these ancient times that people we now call Indians moved into North America from Siberia and spread throughout the continent, leaving behind beautiful rock carvings, paintings and enormous burial mounds. In the dry plateaux of the Southwest there are ancient adobe-built houses and villages perched on cliff-faces, such as Montezuma Castle in New Mexico and Mesa Verde village in Colorado. Although mysteriously abandoned centuries ago, these empty buildings have a haunting, poetic beauty.

Another centuries-old Indian site, still inhabited, is the village of Acoma, built astride a 357 ft flat-topped *mesa* in New Mexico's desert. It was seen, and by-passed, by the first Spanish explorers to visit the region. Clearly impressed, they called it "a great city in the sky ... the strongest position ever seen in the world". The Spaniards came up from Mexico in the early sixteenth century in a vain search for the fabulous gold of the mythical Seven Cities of Cíbola. Instead, they extended their empire in the New World to include the western and southwestern parts of what is now the United States, together with the Florida peninsula.

The Spanish colonists built a network of military garrisons (or *presidios*), missions and ranches, around which huddled small villages (or *pueblos*). Many of these eventually grew into bustling modern cities, such as Los Angeles, San Francisco or San Diego. California and the Southwest thus have a rich legacy of old Spanish buildings, among which are California's missions, the rugged building in San Antonio, Texas, now famous as the Alamo, and the lovely mission of San Xavier del Bac, near Tucson, Arizona.

Meanwhile, other European nations were furthering their interests elsewhere in North America: from their settlements along the St Lawrence River, the French explored the Great Lakes area and the Mississippi Valley. Although they were more interested in the fur trade than in founding an empire, some of their trading posts eventually blossomed into such cities as Chicago, Detroit, Kansas City and St Louis. New Orleans grew from a more ambitious settlement laid out in 1718, which survives as the historic downtown district known as the Vieux Carré, or French Quarter. It is here and in such charming communities as Sainte Genevieve, on the Mississippi River in Missouri, that the French presence is most felt.

The Atlantic coast of America saw bitter rivalry in the seventeenth century between the English, Dutch and Swedes for possession of the continent, a struggle from which the English emerged as the victors. Between the founding of their first colony at Jamestown in 1607 and the outbreak of the Revolutionary War in 1776, the English established 13 settlements along this coast between Maine and Georgia. The last was the colony of Savannah, Georgia, now a gracious historic city of lovely squares laid out in 1733.

Many of the buildings in the colonies, constructed mainly of brick, resembled those of the Georgian style back home in England. Elegant town houses, impressive public buildings and graceful churches

Previous page Mesa Verde National Park, in southwestern Colorado, contains the well-preserved remains of stone dwellings built by Indian peoples long ago. The sites were mysteriously abandoned by the Indians more than two centuries before Christopher Columbus arrived in the New World in 1492.

Below The graceful old Spanish mission of San Xavier del Bac, with its ornate facade and uncompleted white towers, rises from the dry mesquite and sagebrush country south of present-day Tucson, in Arizona. Affectionately known as the "White Dove of the Desert," this beautiful building was constructed by Spanish missionaries and Pima Indian workers between 1783 and 1797.

Right Old white clapboard churches and elegant homes line the streets of Manchester in southern Vermont. This delightful part of New England contains many fine colonial buildings.

embellished with white, columned porticoes and topped with white cupolas and steeples still grace many old eastern towns and cities.

Still standing in the rural districts of the old southern colonies are many magnificent mansions and plantation houses built by rich aristocrats in the seventeenth and eighteenth centuries, notably George Washington's beloved Mount Vernon home beside the Potomac River and others along the James River.

During the nineteenth century, public buildings were constructed in styles of architecture that reflected those currently in favor in Europe, many themselves revivals of earlier fashions. As in the eighteenth century, the inspiration for many American designers was the classical architecture of ancient Greece and Rome, with its elegant columns, pediments and porticoes. Thomas Jefferson had set the tone earlier with his designs for his house Monticello, in Charlottesville, and the Virginia State Capitol, in Richmond. Other architects of the time, such as Benjamin Latrobe, followed the trends and created, in the new Federal style, such magnificent buildings as the National Capitol in Washington DC, on which work began in 1793.

Previous Page Recalling the days when America's eastern seaboard was ruled by the British, skillfully reconstructed old buildings and costumed hosts and hostesses evoke eighteenth century colonial life in Virginia's early capital of Williamsburg. Among the settlement's restored atmospheric inns, apart from the famous Raleigh Tavern, is the charming Wetherburn's Tavern.

Left A close-up look at the magnificent Carson Mansion in Eureka, California, reveals the exquisite craftsmanship of the carpenters who embellished its exterior with Victorian-style decoration in the late nineteenth century. This pleasant old fishing and lumber town, settled around 1850 on California's north coast, contains many such gems of Victorian architecture.

Far Left Many towns and cities sprang up in the West in the late nineteenth century at a time when highly ornamental Victorian-style architecture was in fashion. Among them was the historic silver-mining town of Georgetown, in the Rocky Mountains west of Denver. Here more than 200 Victorian houses have been preserved and restored.

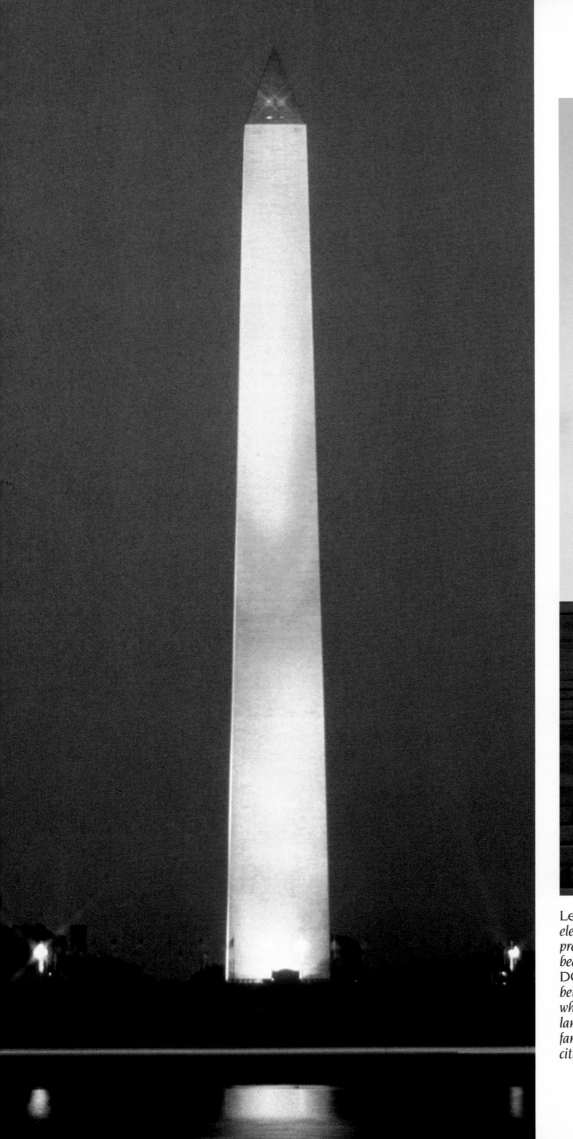

Left   The Washington Monument, an elegant memorial to America's first president, glows like a beacon over the beautiful federal capital of Washington DC when illuminated at night. Built between 1848 and 1884 and faced with white Maryland marble, the gleaming landmark soars 555 ft above other famous public buildings in the heart of the city.

Above   The colossal brooding figure of
President Abraham Lincoln sits inside
the Memorial erected in his honor in
Washington DC. Completed in 1922, the
austere, white marble building suggests a
Greek temple and is particularly
impressive when illuminated at night.

Contrasting sharply with the clean, elegant lines of such classical buildings, an American version of the medieval European Gothic style of architecture was also popular in the nineteenth century. With its pointed forms and encrusted decoration, it was used for many cathedrals and churches, such as St Patrick's Cathedral and Trinity Church in New York.

The later years of the century saw the development of the highly ornamented Victorian style, adopted for many of the gracious homes that still survive in many American cities such as the beautiful houses on Steiner Street in San Francisco. Many smaller houses and cottages across the country are embellished with the effusive Victorian decoration known as "gingerbread".

After the Great Fire of Chicago in 1871, a new method of constructing taller buildings, using steel framing, was adopted for commercial buildings and stores by architects of the renowned Chicago School. Among them was Louis Sullivan, whose Carson, Pirie & Scott store in the Chicago and Guaranty (now Prudential) building in Buffalo were forerunners of the skyscrapers that now soar above modern American city skylines. Another influential architect of these years was Frank Lloyd Wright, whose spacious low private houses and later spiral-shaped Guggenheim Museum in New York are well known.

In the twentieth century the swirling forms of Art Nouveau decoration on buildings of the Chicago School gave way to the more streamlined, angular rhythms of Art Deco, which were applied to many buildings of the 1920s and 1930s. Among the many examples in New York is the magnificent Chrysler Building, whose glittering spire stands out on the city's breathtaking skyline.

Previous Page A battling, working city by day, New York at night becomes a sea of lights as theaters, clubs and restaurants advertize their attractions, people relax in their high-rise apartments and, in some office blocks, a few lonely souls work on far into the night, sending urgent communications all over the globe.

Right The 607 ft Space Needle is a prominent Seattle landmark dominating the cultural and entertainment complex of Seattle Center. This futuristic steel structure, a legacy of the 1962 World's Fair, offers breathtaking panoramas from the observation deck and restaurants at the top.

Below Among the man-made splendors of America is the Chicago city sky line, which boasts the tallest building in America, the Sears Tower. Sunset sees the plate-glass windows reflecting a rosy red, before the towering skyscrapers become a dramatic black silhouette against the evening sky.

The eight-and-a-half-mile long Bay Bridge that links San Francisco with neighboring Oakland leaps in a series of elegant gray spans across San Francisco Bay. Completed in 1936, it is one year older than its more illustrious neighbor, the Golden Gate Bridge.

Seen from the northwest, the wedge-shaped 853 ft Transamerica Pyramid and the 52 story Bank of America Tower stand out on the impressive skyline of San Francisco's bustling financial district. John Steinbeck called this captivating city "a golden handcuff with the key thrown away."

Below The glittering modern office towers of New York's financial district dominate the skyline of Lower Manhattan. The sleek twin towers of the World Trade Center soar to a breathtaking 110 stories. This section of the city is linked to the neighboring borough of Brooklyn by the majestic Brooklyn Bridge, an engineering marvel constructed in 1883 over the East River.

Over the years many other fine structures appeared in towns and cities across the nation. With the spread of the railroads came impressive stations and terminals, none more imposing than New York's Grand Central Station. There are also fine bridges, graceful and elegant, like San Francisco's Golden Gate Bridge, or New York's Brooklyn Bridge, and other engineering marvels with their special kind of beauty, such as the great river dams, notably the Hoover Dam on the Colorado.

In all the great cities magnificent sports stadiums, with their graceful curves, are recognizable landmarks. Some cities, such as Washington DC, have fine modern airports with superb terminal buildings, the most adventurous of which must include the sweeping bird-like structure designed for TWA at New York's Kennedy Airport. Everywhere there are beautiful monuments, ranging from the colossal Shrine of Democracy at

Mount Rushmore to the futuristic curve of the Gateway Arch in St Louis. The beautiful fountains of such cities as Portland, Oregon, and Kansas City, Missouri, have counterparts in many other American cities, all with attractive public parks; some, such as Boston, Buffalo and New York, boast parks laid out by the celebrated Frederick Law Olmsted.

Since World War II, many old city centers, once the scene of urban decay, have been skillfully renovated and revitalized with exciting new buildings, plazas, fountains and sculptures. Magnificent new office and hotel skyscrapers, designed by such world-famous architects as Mies van der Rohe, I.M. Pei and John Portman, now grace the soaring futuristic skylines of many downtown districts.

The rejuvenated cities, the stunning natural scenery and the fascinating wildlife are visible proof that America is, and will remain, a beautiful land.

PICTURE CREDITS